The publisher and the author make no guarantees concerning the level
of success you may experience by following the advice and strategies
contained within this book, and you accept that results will differ for
each individual. The testimonials and examples provided in this book
describe unique experiences, which may not apply to the reader, and
therefore the same outcomes may not be achieved. The views are that
of the author alone and intends to only inform and enlighten readers
through a personal story.

Copyright © 2021 Liam Mistry
All rights reserved

Preface

April 2021

Within each of us lies an answer to a better and healthier future. Clinical trials provide a path to those answers. Helping to bring new or improved treatments a step closer to those who need them is why I decided to play a role in an industry that is taking us all to a place of hope and cure.

The idea for this book came from the realisation that through working in this exciting industry, I could share my journey, insights, stories and personal perspective, at a suitable stage, with those who want to share in this vision of living in a healthier world.

You could benefit from this book if:
- *You want a unique insight into clinical research*
- *You aspire to join the industry*
- *You want top tips and useful information.*

I also intend for this book to serve as a reminder for myself of the exciting and busy phase in my career, through what I would describe as being on the 'critical path' for fully appreciating the inner workings of major research environments the challenges of transitioning between them and how they all relate to each other.

I often get asked questions about my experience and found some common themes, therefore I have tried to address some of these. This book is intended to be a personal account based on particular highlights within my own experience, and with that in mind it is important to consider that any views are that of my own.

I would like to thank friends and family who have supported me on my journey to date and to those who have taken the time to read my book.

Author, Liam Mistry RICR
BSc.(Hons) Biomedical Science,
MSc Healthcare Policy & Management

Contents

Introduction 1

Chapter 1- The Clinical Research Site.3

Getting through the door 4

Connecting with your team & getting the full site experience 7

The Gloomy Office 9

The Lightbulb Moment 12

Blues and Two's -Times up! 15

Top Tips 17

Chapter 2 – Working at a Contract Research Organisation 20

Escaping to the other side 21

Spinning Plates 23

The Clinical Lead & so-called 'Study Team'.............26

The Power of Matrix Management 29

The Sponsor 32

Top Tips 35

Chapter 3 – Working for a Clinical Trial Sponsor ...38

Jumping over yet another fence ...39

Cruising at 37,000ft ...41

Going Big or Going Small ...44

Back to the drawing board ...46

All the eyes are on you ...48

Top Tips ...50

Chapter 4 – Being a Clinical Research Associate (CRA) ...53

Why become a CRA? ...54

"But it's impossible to get my first CRA Job" ...57

Once I am a CRA it will be plain sailing ...60

Have your passports and suitcases ready ...63

Top Tips ...67

Chapter 5 – Healthcare in the Community & Beyond ...70

Chapter 6 – Perks, pathways and specialist functions ...75

Clinical Operations ...77

Data Management ...78

Medical Affairs 79

Regulatory Affairs 80

Pharmacovigilance 80

Logistics & Supplies 81

Business Development & Management 82

Chapter 7 – Where next, and the future of the clinical research industry .84

Chapter 8 – The Patient 87

Glossary 92

Introduction

The clinical research industry boasts innovation, trials and ground-breaking science, in relation to therapies and healthcare products. I have worked in this industry for several years and have been fortunate to be a part of clinical research roles, working from within different environments that interwork to drive a product from the lab bench to the bedside. I explore these areas in more detail from a personal viewpoint focusing on the highlights of my experiences.

For anyone unsure of the overall process of drug discovery, the way in which a new drug is brought to market can be both complex and time consuming. New products could be in a development stage for over 10 years and still fail crucial tests to allow them to get into market. Typically, it all starts with lab discovery work, which involves testing new compounds as candidates and tweaking them as knowledge is gained for optimum effectiveness. After this stage, these candidates are tested on animals and significant data is generated to aid the viability of a chosen product for human trials. These stages are classified as the pre-clinical stages.

Following this, the potential drug is tested for the first time in humans. This starts the clinical stage of drug development which comprises of mainly three phases. In phase 1 trials, depending on the product it can be tested on healthy volunteers, or in the case for a cancer drug for example, this may be given to patients with the disease who need life saving treatment options. If successful, the trials will progress to phase 2 and then phase 3. During the process the safety, effectiveness and efficiency of the drug is tested in increasingly larger populations. Sometimes phase 4 post marketing studies are conducted to test the ongoing safety and effectiveness of a new drug

If a drug is shown to be effective and safe, regulatory authorities and healthcare providers will commission it for use. This area is an entirely separate and complex field which requires specialist skills and qualification. For example, a MSc in Healthcare Policy and Management will provide a good baseline to understand this area.

I will share my story of working at a clinical research site, the struggles of finding my first role and the challenges and triumphs in between. I turn to focus on my experience within a Contract Research Organisation (CRO) and my time working for a clinical trial sponsor. My perspective will hopefully shine a light on the key differences noticed as I moved through each research environment. The tips that have been included are ones that I often refer to. I will also cover my insights into various departments within the industry, working as a Clinical Research Associate (CRA) and share my story on healthcare in the community and beyond. Finally, I provide a spin on where I think the industry is heading in the future and of course not forgetting the patient.

Chapter 1- The Clinical Research Site

Getting through the door

Little did I know where my career would end up. On one hand, as a car enthusiast, the prospect of working in engineering, vehicle design or dealerships became a real possibility. On the other hand, I also loved the world of aviation so that did not seem like a bad option either. But what I really felt a drive for were careers that made a real difference to people's health and with a natural ability in science it became a no brainer to pursue a career in clinical research.

Navigating your way through the many avenues and entry points into the clinical research industry can be challenging. There are so many different specialties within the field due to the complex and global scale at which new drug trials are carried out. Getting a job at a clinical research site is perhaps a good starting point since it gives you the opportunity to see things on the ground; from nurses administering trial medication to patients desperately needing new options, the doctors scrambling to make ends meet, often juggling many different priorities and not to forget the logistical and operational circus are all things that keep sites ticking along.

So, where do you begin? Well, the first place to look is on the website of the local hospitals or clinics near to you. For me, as I live in the UK this was the National Health Service (NHS) jobs website. Setting up alerts for jobs containing keywords such as "Clinical Research" or "Clinical Trial" would allow me to filter out the roles I was after. I often searched outside of my local area for jobs just to see how common the roles were and the types available if I were daring enough to move location at the time. After many days of searching, one Friday night at 9pm I stumbled across a role for a Project Assistant on page 23 of the website. Yes, those very details I can still remember! It was at a hospital within an hour of where I lived and seemed to tick all the boxes. It was an entry level role for 2 years that came with a sponsored part time masters programme in healthcare and was designed for graduates just like me at the time. Without hesitation I applied and later received a first stage interview.

The day came when I had to give a first stage interview presentation about the NHS and what it meant to me. I recall talking with five or six other candidates at the time in the waiting area and got to know them and thought to myself they would make great colleagues should I be successful. Unfortunately, I did not make the cut out from the hundreds of people they had called for the first stage. Yes, the competition was high! So, there I was, back on the job websites again. Only a few weeks later I stumbled across the same role, except this time it was advertised within another department at the same hospital. I was in two minds to apply but since my original application was already saved, I thought "why not!". I'm glad I did! This time I received an invitation for a direct interview a few days later.

Little did I know the role was for the same programme for which funding had just been released to open more positions but due to time constraints, they abolished the multi-step interviewing process. I got to speak directly to the head of the programme as well as current employees and had the opportunity to describe my experience to date. After being collected from reception by the interviewer and having a good chat in some detail about my experience along the way to the interview room, I distinctly remember the interviewer commenting "I think we've had the interview already". This made me feel comfortable and subsequently the interview went well. I was later offered the first-choice area of liver research to work in, alongside one of the top professors in the field. By the way, the people I met at the initial interview were also successful and we started on the programme together. Its strange how things turn out!

Connecting with your team & getting the full site experience

After onboarding at any new workplace, familiarising yourself with the coffee machine buttons and the canteen menu, it'll be time to get down to some real work. I remember being part of a large team with nurses, trial coordinators, medical fellows and administrators. It felt like there was a constant revolving door with team members coming in and out of the office, some of whom I had not yet introduced myself to. I would overhear conversations about the work they were doing and the patients that they had seen. It all seemed a million miles away from the comfortable office we were in. I wanted to see things for myself and experience the real clinical trial work going on at the front line.

It was at this point that it was key to get to know the team better, so that I could be invited along to their clinics and help with some of their errands. My mentor at the time advised that it would be beneficial for me to acknowledge and get to know as many people that I crossed paths with as this could potentially open doors for me one day. This technique would make sure I was recognised amongst the wider team. I took this advice on board and soon found myself delivering paperwork to clinics in the main hospital, picking up lab samples from the labs and going to the university research unit. This additional work allowed me to interact with different team members and get a broader understanding of how the hospital worked.

A nurse was involved in a liver transplant study which used a special machine to keep livers active with a blood supply whilst outside the body and allowed surgeons to test the function of the organ before it was transplanted. She offered for me to go and watch a live operation if I wanted to. I took up the offer and found myself one day inside an operating theatre at an arms distance from the patient, watching world class surgeons perform life saving surgery.

In a similar scenario, I took up the opportunity to attend clinical multi disciplinary meetings with the consultants and was asked to take the lead on a small project to collect real world data on a new drug recently approved. This was to see if the results were comparable to trial results. It also meant I got to present the findings at a Royal College of Physicians conference.

Working near patients, doctors and clinical staff made finding opportunities very easy, and being at the heart of medicine meant that I could start telling real stories back in the office about what I had seen and done. I learnt how making connections with people in the wider team really can bring home experiences that you thought would not be achievable.

The Gloomy Office

The site office you may find yourself working in is much different to that you may find in a non-clinical environment. What a surprise I had when I arrived on my first day to a small gloomy office! It was dark, super stuffy, had a small window right near the ceiling and not to forget the clinical smells which was something to get use to. I could almost touch both sides of the office walls with my arms stretched out wide and since there were three desks, this room had to be shared with others. I kept my focus in the work at hand and did not see this as any barrier, but could not help feeling like I had pulled the short straw, knowing that my colleagues were working in a brand-new refurbished research building at the other end of the hospital.

Nurses would come in and out for information during the day, but being in an isolated office most of the time, staring at the clock occasionally kept me alert! Winter was the worst period when it would get dark early and I hardly saw the daylight. It was my mission to improve my experience so I decided to start taking lunches in the new building where I would be able to interact with the other graduates. This helped to the point where I asked my manager if I could work an afternoon per week at the hot desks. Although reluctant, she agreed and gradually I was beginning to get the best of both worlds. Soon I was to find out that there were plans to move us over to the new building later in the year which was a big relief.

One thing about working in a research office, is that you forget that the patient is literally next door. You can go from sitting with your coffee on your comfy desk chair, to seeing real trauma, suffering and pandemonium within seconds. This was exciting and brought home the message that the work I was involved with really mattered. Discussions would all be about the patient, what they did, how they were and what the plan was. The real reason I chose to work at the site came to life and the gloomy office started to feel miles away.

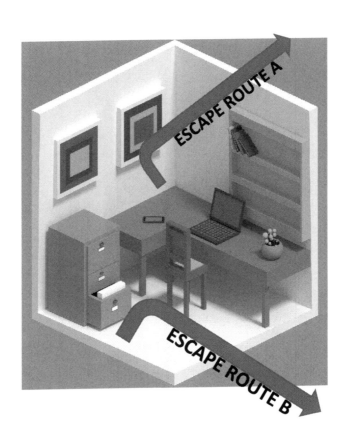

The Lightbulb Moment

One of the biggest characteristics of conducting research is the continuous monitoring of the trial data, ensuring that the trial quality and safety of patients is upheld. Clinical Research Associates (CRAs) play a huge role in this and travel to clinical investigator sites to review how the trial is going and to help to resolve any issues. It wasn't too long before I met the CRAs who would be working with me. Initially, I did not know anything about who they where or what they did but remember being told that certain up to date documents were needed and someone would come to visit me. The concept of what CRAs did soon became familiar to me and was important to my day to day activities and follow up work at the site.

The person I worked with lived locally but used to travel to other sites across the UK, each time they visited I saw it as an opportunity to learn about what they did...and of course as an excuse to escape the gloomy office! I used to spend the day shadowing them in the so called "monitoring room" where associates from different companies used to sit to review the study files. I found out about the role and how the travel was for them. The thought of being able to get company benefits like a company car, expenses and private healthcare were the perks I was looking for in my career and the ability to travel with work was something I had always wanted to do. All this, together with a position which was closely linked to the site and was a progressive step from my role at that time. It was not always a glamorous job. Often, they would be away from home a couple of days at a time, sit in small, cramped areas with little or no natural light and be left to work without seeing anyone for most of the day – it reminded me of something! I recall there being office chat about who was coming in, depending on how much the nurses liked them would determine if they got the 'nice room with the window' or the 'dark and small room far away from the office'. It was clear that the key to success was getting on well with the site teams. I certainly made it my mission to make the visitors feel welcome.

I realised that although working at site was great, clinical research is global in nature and was certainly not restricted to one hospital or country. I wanted to experience getting out and about with my role. I was asked to take on some work with one of the consultants who did not have much time on their hands, surprise surprise! They had won a grant from a large company to carry out research on the real-life data of a new drug which had recently been licenced after successful clinical trials. I took the lead on this and worked with different hospitals in the UK to gather data, analyse and present it. We managed to get a slot at a Royal College of Physicians event to showcase the results and being the lead, I had to go to present to a room of enthusiastic consultants. This was one of the highlights of my time working at site as I had gone from being stuck in the small gloomy office to presenting on the big stage in front of leading doctors in the field. I finally got to travel, and it gave me the motivation to continue doing such things.

At the bottom of a confirmation letter received for a monitoring visit that was coming up, I saw that it had been written by someone who had the same job title as me. It surprised me as it was impossible to find a similar position in a pharmaceutical company during my graduate job searches, yet the proof was in front of me that such roles did exist. I had obviously missed something and stared at it for a good while in shock! After discovering that there was a world of opportunity outside of the site and started frantically searching for these positions online. There was not a single opening found. It was only when I mentioned this to the CRA visiting me that they revealed that many roles in research were outsourced to Contract Research Organisations (CROs) and they gave me the names of the top five. Later that week I uncovered a new world of opportunity and thought to myself "if only I had known this before". There were more roles than I could think to imagine.

I had a lightbulb moment!

Blues and Two's -Times up!

One thing I knew for sure before joining the site, was that I had limited time there, as I was given a fixed term contract and shortly after starting to work there, I began to understand why. Much of the funding that comes into a research department is from the payments that drug companies make to sites to carry out the work on their product, including overheads. This money eventually builds up and allows site departments to fund posts for a certain number of years with the hope that they can extend the contract at the end, provided there is sufficient funding and a business need. Either way, I am not the sort of person who likes the idea of not knowing where my employment status will be every 24 months, so it was something I could not tolerate but I ventured on.

The team I worked for knew my contract was nearing an end and were desperate to keep me on. I was offered a Clinical Trial Coordinator role, but many of the duties were the same as what I had already been doing. Although there were multiple other roles I could explore at the site, I wanted to head for the bright lights of this industry, but that meant leaving my hometown and moving to the South where these companies were based. I remember feeling like it was an emergency to find a new role, with the constant sound of the clock ticking and sirens ringing in my head of my contract starting to run out. I did not anticipate how much of a challenge it was to jump from a site to industry as many of the positions wanted industry experience, or that you had to have previously used certain systems. I remember taking days off where I would drive long distances for interviews and then sometimes having to go back the following week. Once I remember having two interviews with one company only a week apart, talk about Déjà vu!

At last, I had finally been invited for an interview at a company that I had applied to many times before but had never heard back from. It really paid to keep trying! I had spent quality time researching the company and the role as well as what was expected. I had to give a presentation on Good Clinical Practice (GCP) and its practical applications, then did a competency-based interview. Little did I know that the interviewer had visited my site many times when they were a CRA, and we spent some time discussing that. He also knew one of the managers, then to my surprise offered that we should call them right there and then! I was given their business card and asked to pass it on when I got back to site. The nervous wait began. Then a few days later, I heard that my interviewer had called my colleague and had a discussion, it was at this point I realised what a small world clinical research was and that there really was a close connection between companies and hiring managers beyond all those automated job application systems. I finally received the offer that I had got the position based in Reading, UK and I was over the moon. My time was up at site, finally the sirens were silenced, and the clock went back to normal. I was ready to embark on a career outside of the site!

Top Tips

#1 - Always work at site with an open mind, things change often, and your environment will not always be pleasant.

#2 - Due to the vast number of specialities and people working within any one site, make as much contact as possible. Even if this means saying hello to someone as you pass them in the corridor, you never know when you will require their expertise so it's good to get recognised.

#3 - The most dull and boring tasks can lead to the biggest and greatest experiences. Collecting data or assisting a consultant with a mundane task may seem boring at first, but sometimes these are linked to a wider project which you will eventually get an opportunity to get more involved with and can lead to great things, trips and presentations.

#4 - Ask questions. By questioning things that you are unsure of, or new to, will allow you to understand more about how these fit into the bigger picture. Often sites are working on multiple projects at any one time and at different stages, so it is good to be able to map out these in linear order to understand the site process.

#5 - Make the most of every visit to the site by a CRA or external guest. Often these people can offer great advice and insight into their roles or

17

experiences. Many people gain places in industry through referrals, so it is always good to maintain a good relationship.

#6 – Do not be afraid to ask for experiences that you might not think you will get. If you want to watch a surgery, shadow a clinic, or even spend time with a ward manager it really is just a question away. The privilege of working in a site already will mean that it is much easier to gain experience in different areas if permitted.

#7 – Use contract terms to your advantage. If you find that your contract is coming to an end soon do not panic. Often if you have shown that you are a great worker then the chances are that the employer will do all they can to keep you on. It is also a great way to begin discussions early on about progression and development opportunities.

#8 – Make use of the training on offer. As sites have many busy accredited professionals working at them, personal development courses can often be run locally to save travel time for staff. They are also often open to all employees, so it is a great way to learn new skills and attend courses that are relevant for your development.

#9 – Keep in mind that you work in a very busy, patient centred environment. It is always important to act professionally and to respect the patients and visitors as you work in these areas. Some of them may not be going through the best of times.

#10 – Enjoy the highs and lows of site life, it really is fulfilling. Even days that are tough or hard will give you something to feel great about as well as those days that make working at site fun.

Chapter 2 – Working at a Contract Research Organisation

Escaping to the other side

The sun was shining, I had just moved to my riverside flat on the banks of the River Thames, and I was in a plush new office situated in a leafy business park. Waking up and going to work on my first day at a CRO was a great feeling and I was finally on the other side of the fence, it felt like I had escaped the chaos of the site.... or so I thought.

When working at a site you become accustomed to taking orders from the CRO or sponsor running the trial and completing things according to their guidance. I knew that my previous experience would come in very handy. There were so many times that I could think back to when I was at site where I thought about how CROs could do things differently, and if only I had the privilege to do so. When meeting new colleagues and listening to some of their frustrations it was clear that they had never worked at site and could not grasp the concept of the busy, chaotic and patient centred environment that their site teams were working in. I was asked along with another new starter to give a presentation about life in the NHS and at site during my first weeks. It was great; we decided to do a role play of some typical scenes and scenarios to highlight the challenges that many site staff face each day. It was a real laugh to enact some stereotypical characteristics of roles in the industry.

Working in a CRO brought with it some surprises. The vast amount of training that you must complete during the first few weeks was incredible.

There were more than a hundred training modules and procedures to read then on top of all of that there was study specific training. I found it strange when it came to the point of contacting a site for the first time and knew that a good first impression was key to a successful site relationship. I imagined calling myself in my previous role, after all, if it was the nice monitoring room with the window that was desired one day, this was important. As I knew there was a close-knit community within clinical research, it meant that my colleague next to me was contacting my old manager and site team for the study she was working on. I remember telling her to say "Hi from me" each time she was on the phone to them. It really highlighted the different side of the fence that I was now working on. It was time to give instructions to site, get to grips with the study and after completing the mountain of training I finally felt comfortable dealing with sites from the other side.

Spinning Plates

If there was one thing that anyone working in a CRO will comment on, it is the constant feeling of having to spin many plates. Often you are working on multiple projects with different clients at different stages. In one moment, I would be arranging a site visit and in the next I could be reviewing a Trial Master File in preparation for a study termination or picking up the phone to firefight a site issue. The ability to keep a well organised and clear mind is crucial to succeeding in this environment and even more so, its important as you will be monitored like a hawk on your metrics.

I was fortunate to work at two of these organisations, and both were very similar in their set up and operation. At the time when I joined my first one, the ability to tell sites what to do felt great, that was until I discovered that the client, a.k.a sponsor, also instructed them what to do. You feel trapped in the middle a lot of the time, with the client requesting one thing and the site telling you another. That is when it occurred to me that the role of a CRO is to guide and direct best practice on both sides to ensure that both deliverables are met, and the site teams can work with a solution that suits them.

Another aspect to the 'spinning plates' environment of a CRO is that there are numerous departments that you need to interact with. There are regulatory teams, study start up teams, monitoring, medical and many others. At times I thought "why aren't there fewer departments and interdependencies?" After some time working in another organisation with less structure, I realised why. In my view, CROs are like the fast-food chains of the clinical research world. Customers place their orders, want a service quickly, on time and as described at a good price. When I began to dig deeper, I realised that segmentation was the key to success in this analogy. In a fast-food chain, there usually is one person whose role it is to take orders, another person just makes fries, whilst another team member's role is to make the burgers. If that hasn't made you feel hungry already, then at the end all the components are bagged together to satisfy the customer's order...but in the meantime a further ten orders have racked up. Its no different for a CRO, and because they do not own physical products, most of their revenue comes from an emphasis on creating new business and providing increased service.

With responsibility comes order and structure. At the end of the day, any new product will need to stand up not just to regulatory requirements but the demand for quality from the clients too. I was not accustomed to all the additional admin, forms and tracking in place to begin with, however after a while it became second nature. There is even a tracker for trackers and a single piece of information is usually reported in at least three different places. Although it felt like a pain at times, the importance of this became apparent later in my career.

I remember often coming to work and hearing buzz words such as 'metrics', 'days on site', 'QC issues', 'book to bill' ringing in my ears each day, so much so sometimes that I found it easy to lose track of the trial, the patients and the reality of what I was doing. As a naturally organised person I liked the fact that order and structure was enforced so much. I remember some colleagues struggling with this and the talk of inheriting a 'bad' study was something always lingering over everyone's shoulders. Overall, once you are into the swing of things, a CRO is a busy, fast paced, fun and dynamic environment and this buzz really is something that you should not miss to experience.

The Clinical Lead & so-called 'Study Team'

When it comes to working at a CRO, the person that you will work with a lot of the time is the Clinical Lead. They are usually responsible for the clinical and operational management of a study across a region. Sometimes there are Global Clinical Leads and as their title suggests they would oversee the operational aspects of a study globally for larger studies. There are also the additional project leads and managers who collectively form the so called 'study team'. I realised just how top heavy a study team could become and this starts to explain where some of the challenges could stem from.

I remember being introduced to my projects and hearing about the 'study team' from my manager. Often it was like waiting for the lottery results to come up because it was just so random as to what type of team you would be working with, and most importantly who your Clinical Lead would be. Often the leads I worked with were based in a different country to myself and were working on multiple studies at any one time. The reason why leads are so important is because they dictate the direction of the study and some of your activities at the country and site level, so getting on well with them and having someone who is on the ball is a distinct advantage.

There was a time when I was called to rescue a really challenging study with tight timelines and deadlines to be met. The study had already missed some milestones and the pressure was on to get the sites up and running. The first question I asked myself was, why has it got to this stage? Surely with all the Clinical Leads, Project Managers and Directors this should have been managed. The answer was simple – there was a lack of clear communication, definition of roles and responsibility, all sprinkled with a lack of strategy. These components are vital to ensure Clinical Leads can operate with the local teams effectively and it is equally as important for anyone interacting with the study team to bear this in mind. At times it was like being asked to tune a car's radio whilst its wheels were still not fitted when it came to strategy to activate the sites, and at other times there were more emails to read than there were hours in the day. Thankfully, situations like these are rare, but individuals have unique styles of working, so the key to success was in really finding a way to work with each Clinical Lead, to not be afraid to question, suggest and justify my point of view and approach to the work. In the end a new strategy, better communication and clearly defining the responsibilities pulled the study out of the grave and it was as simple as that!

It's not all doom and gloom however, I have worked with some fantastic study teams. They make working in a CRO a joy. With many processes and procedures, there really is a fine balance with how much a Clinical Lead communicates and interacts with you. Too much and it becomes overwhelming with no space to think, too little and someone could easily drift to working on other priorities and studies. As for Project Managers and Study Directors, the site focussed teams have little interaction with them as those roles are primarily client facing. They often deal with project financials, budgeting and liaising with the clients to keep them informed of progress. All in all, when a site team needed my help, or I was unsure and had to escalate something, there was always a phrase that would save the day - "let me check with the study team".

The Power of Matrix Management

One thing which I found was a distinct advantage of working in such a multi-departmental organisation was the level of dedication in any one functional area. Take for example the line management function. At site, my manager was a nurse, study manager, a data coordinator as well as study coordinator. In comparison at a CRO, my line manager was just that, which meant that I received dedicated one-to-one support with my work at any given time. This shift was a difficult concept to grasp at first, but as time went on it was clear that there were different mindsets required when dealing with company, HR and development tasks compared with working with study teams on clinical trials.

A simple way to explain the concept of matrix management within a CRO is by drawing out a grid. Imagining that for each staff member, each column represents a study, the row would represent the Functional or Line Manager. The Clinical Leads would manage your work vertically, overseeing each specific trial, whereas the Managers would oversee all of your trials but not any particular one of them i.e. manage your work horizontally.

As I began getting into this dual mode style of management, I began to realise how powerful it was in ensuring the best experience as an employee in a CRO. Often, I would hear friends talk about how their managers had no time to discuss development areas or felt they could not speak out because their line managers were also their project lead. The more time I spent in CROs meant that my mind also started to think in terms of organised sections. As well as project responsibilities, it was clear that I also equally had company, development and training responsibilities which should be given the same level of effort and attention. This concept would remain engrained with me going forward in my career.

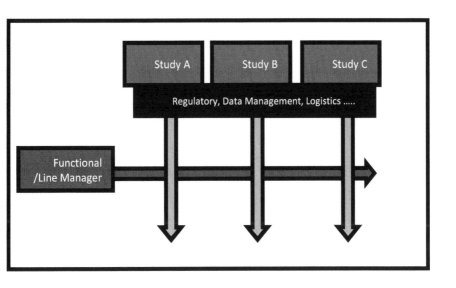

The Sponsor

The first time I heard about the word 'sponsor' I wondered who was running a race for charity. Little did I know this is the common term used to describe the company who are running and funding a clinical trial, and whose drug or device is being tested. This could be a big pharmaceutical giant, or a smaller biotechnology company; either way the sponsors are responsible for the conduct and accountability of any given study they are running regardless of whether it is being run through a CRO or not.

I remember that the sponsor was always made out to be the king or queen of the clinical trial arena, whereby they had the power and the authority to say and do as they wished. In contrast I was bound to set procedures and ways of working and quickly found one of the biggest challenges was trying to bend and flex to the sponsor's requirements whilst keeping my cool when trying to follow the often-complex multi-step processes within a CRO. It was no wonder I always overheard people dreaming of a life working at a sponsor organisation. I can recall the common conversations of "It will be so much more relaxed" ..." you can make your own deadlines", the talk goes on. One advantage that CROs have over sponsors is the weighting towards a specialism in running clinical trials and the operational expertise to navigate the complex regulatory and clinical challenges within the industry. After all, if a sponsor had the sheer resource required to fully run a study themselves, they would not outsource to such organisations.

Over time I was fortunate to work with many different sponsors. Some large and some small, but each of them had their unique ways of working. There were the sponsors who would request we use all their forms and procedures, whereas others would barely make a request and let you work with greater autonomy. The smaller sponsors tend to be more hands on with their approach and sometimes I had direct contact with them for certain tasks. I found that it was the smaller organisations who gave me the most experience and fair share of challenges too, all of which ensured I could develop the skills I needed to progress. Often there was chat amongst colleagues as to which sponsor they got to work with, and due to the high turnover of staff and projects, it was common for handovers to take place between different team members. Sometimes studies and sponsors gained an internal reputation and it became the 'talk of the town'.

It was common to meet the sponsor occasionally when visiting site. They would often conduct oversight visits and check compliance. If dealing with the sponsor through a screen was enough pressure, the visits sometimes felt intensive with the representatives watching your every move. I must say, it is not all as bad as that. Most of the time the sponsors are a pleasure to work with and they often have been through the different career stages as yourself so understand the work you do in a CRO. Nowadays, they have adopted functional service provider models with sponsors whereby you work directly with them in their offices but remain employed by the CRO. In this sense, the sponsor has almost become synonymous with them. As trials get more complex and sponsors get more financially savvy, the outsourcing of trials will inevitably grow, and there will be no getting away from that. Little did I know at this point that I would re-visit and work for one of the sponsors whom I dealt with at a later point in my career. As they say it really is a small world in clinical trials.

Top Tips

#1 - Be prepared for a big shake up in the environment. If you are entering a CRO from site, from a sponsor or even as part of your first role, the busy, demanding and fast paced environment is really something to be prepared for.

#2 - Do not let the feeling of power get the best of you. Although you may feel like you can tell sites what tasks need completing or following up with, does not mean that you should be demanding, forceful or disrespectful of their time.

#3 - You will spend much time communicating internally within the CRO as well as externally with sites or sponsors. Each requires its own unique style and its important that you remember the environments that each of your contacts works in to figure out the best way to get the most from them.

#4 - Keep organised. It is important that you keep organised with the different tasks that you need to complete since you will be working on multiple projects at once. It really pays to know what is going on with your studies and sites.

#5 - Do not be afraid to voice your opinions to the study teams. If you feel a process should be changed or that there is a better way to do something, then letting them or management know about it will potentially benefit you as well as the project. Good ideas are always welcomed.

#6 - Always make time to speak about your development and projects with your line manager. CROs are unique in that often you will get a dedicated line manager to talk to about your projects, training and skills. Use this time wisely and make the most of the attention.

#7 - Sponsors will always want more; it is down to you and the project teams to advise and set expectations. After all, CROs are viewed as big machines that churn out results for sponsors and it is often tempting for sponsors to be demanding so always set those boundaries.

#8 - Working in a CRO can often feel overwhelming, process driven and robotic. With research now expanding to new horizons with more work being outsourced to them, its not uncommon to experience greater workloads or pressures. Take it all in your stride and gain the most out of the opportunities you have.

#9 - Often CROs have functional service provisions with sponsors, this means you can remain employed by them, but work dedicated to a particular sponsor. This is a great way and avenue to explore if you want to gain experience working for a sponsor.

#10 - There are so many departments within a CRO so make sure you make the most of them. Do not be afraid to reach out to other team members, spend time shadowing or speaking to them about their work. It can be crazy the amount of information you can gain from a conversation about their day whilst making a coffee.

Chapter 3 – Working for a Clinical Trial Sponsor

Jumping over yet another fence

After having worked in a **CRO** for over three years, in a fast paced and collaborative environment, I could not help but wonder what it would be like to work for a sponsor company. After all, I had heard all the stories but wanted to experience for myself and fully understand how things worked on the 'other side'.

It was difficult to find a role at a sponsor firm, mainly because they often required more experienced staff. Quite commonly their job descriptions stated the number of years' experience that was needed as well as the sort of background expected of the candidate – for example to have worked in a **CRO** with five years experience in industry. I was also very careful to plan which role to move to, since the number and variety of specific roles would not be as broad as with that of a **CRO**, primarily because of the leaner structure that most sponsors operate under. Nonetheless, there were still options for me and sooner or later the perfect role came up at a small company for a Clinical Trial Manager role. It felt like I had scored a hattrick and I was over the moon!

At the time I knew that the move would result in working in a very different way to what I had been used to. Before, there was a great focus on delivery, whereas a sponsor's focus would be more on strategy, planning and having the goal of getting the drug to market as quickly as possible with the highest quality data. The switch in mindset would be akin to when I moved out of the site. I would go from a very structured, set way of doing tasks, to a very open approach to work, with fewer deliverables but increased responsibility and decision-making ability. The sponsor I was moving to was a much smaller firm, so I knew there would be additional challenges such as working in an environment with processes that were still under development and working within smaller teams. It certainly didn't take much time to meet most of the staff and hear their stories - good and bad!

I was excited to say the least to finally being able to complete the circle of seeing, working and appreciating a clinical trial from the perspectives of the inner workings of a site, through to the machinery of a CRO and then to the beacon of the sponsor, even if, at times packing and unpacking desks was becoming a regular activity.

Cruising at 37,000ft

One of the noticeable changes when moving to a sponsor to perform a trial management function, was a switch in the perspective of a study. Working with sites, or being at site and dealing with those on the ground was fascinating and the intricacies of completing certain tasks was sometimes mind boggling. When overseeing a trial run by a CRO and sites, the granular details become somewhat of a distant memory and the day-to-day work becomes more planned and focussed.

When I was a CRA flying over to a remote site, I often looked out of the window to see the landscape and the bigger picture. Cars on the road would appear like ants and the bustling activity on the ground was not to be heard or seen in any detail. Similarly, the sponsor perspective was a change, and I was able to appreciate the complexity and challenge of running a trial but from a bird's eye view. I was accustomed to physically seeing site staff, the site binders and files as well as patient notes, but suddenly, my view had turned two dimensional and I now had to visualise the activity of the study through excel spreadsheets, numerous trackers and metrics. It was certainly something to get used to. The ability to translate the data into real world action plans and to be able to imagine the situation on the ground was a skill that took a little while to learn.

One thing about flying is that you do not realise the speed at which you are travelling, things appear to move slower than you think and the same can be said for working in the trial management function. The pace felt considerably slower, primarily because the tasks that I had to complete were of much greater significance and involved more thought, attention and time to complete. I realised that maybe that is where the whole "it's more relaxed at a sponsor" phrase came from? It was satisfying for me to be able to really focus on a task and think deeply about it. Working at a sponsor also means more oversight, and with that comes the opportunity to still go on site visits to accompany the CRO staff, depending on your role. The excitement and buzz of being at site once more really brings back with it a sense of what your role entails. The relevance of the work I was doing resonated once more. This helped me to focus my attention on what really mattered whilst I was sat in my comfy chair with a cup of coffee far away from the region, sites and teams I was managing.

Having worked my way through the different layers starting from the very front line, meant that I could draw a line right the way through from my current position down to the patients and communities that the work I did affected. It really helped with decision making and found that I often took more time to consider my actions compared to others who had not come to the sponsor with the same background, as I was always thinking about what things would look like for the CRO, sites and patients. In fact it felt like I was cruising at 37,000ft, with some turbulence thrown in along the way of course!

Going Big or Going Small

Often there is debate about the difference between biotechnology companies and pharmaceutical companies. As far as I knew, pharmaceutical companies traditionally made products that had a chemical base, whereas biotechnology companies used a mixture of methods with origins from other living sources and sometimes involved technical engineering to transform them into products. The truth is, nowadays the lines are slightly blurred, and many companies use both methods to form their pipelines; they can even be referred to as Biopharma's just to add to the confusion.

I remember having the option to choose between two job offers when moving to a sponsor. Both were for a similar role in infectious diseases, one was working for a large pharmaceutical giant and the other was to work for a growing small company. I found myself thinking of the two different experiences that I could potentially have. With the larger company it would have been like what I had experienced previously; a host of processes to follow, robust procedures and corporate culture. On the flip side, I had never worked for a smaller expanding company and I had heard that due to the size, structure and sheer complexity of trials often you are given much more of a challenging role in an ever-changing environment. Being someone who wanted good job security, one thing that was always putting me off going to a smaller "one product pipeline"

44

company at the time was that if the trials were ever to fail then the risks for me losing my job would be higher. Nonetheless, it was a risk worth taking since after all I was still at an early stage in my career. I do not regret it!

From starting, to onboarding, to training, the pace was always fast, the process was not always there, and it was usually for me to invent or to write them. As for the trial – it really was all hands to the deck. I found myself getting involved with all things A to Z of clinical trials, on top of doing tasks which were part of developing the corporate and company culture and practices. I was on high adrenaline, and though some of the tasks were things I was doing for the first time, it really was about using logic, getting something to a 'nearly ready' status and then consulting with experts to make finishing touches, all whilst increasing my knowledge along the way. Working for a small company is really something that everyone should experience as it gets you to think hard about what a clinical trial entails, how important each component of it is and how your actions have a direct impact on the study results.

Watch out for a whole range of change too. I was told that the only constant in clinical research is change. With that in mind, I prepared myself prior to joining a smaller company to accept that change was inevitable. From new hires to organisational announcements and changes, no two weeks were the same. At times it felt like being out of my depth, but staying positive and seeing the light at the end of the tunnel is all it takes to get by.

Back to the drawing board

I quickly learnt and experienced as being part of the sponsor that my activities changed in nature, especially within the trial management function. The level of decision making increased ten-fold and there really was nobody else to send things for approval to, which I had been used to for so long. I was now a key member of the 'study team' however this time I was the only person that could really get myself out of challenging situations. I was expected to make my own decisions and use experience to make judgments. One thing that I learnt about decision making was that it was not necessarily a difficult thing all the time, it was the fact that from my previous experience, these kinds of activities seemed so distant, so procedural and so high up the chain that I did not feel the responsibility bearing down on me – I suppose it was a good thing as I was never in a rush to just sign something off without giving it some good thought.

Work at a site or at a CRO was mainly task oriented, whereas at the sponsor the activities were very strategic at times. Often, I would be mapping out a process or designing a strategy to increase recruitment of patients to the study, and be reviewing regulatory guidelines to formulate plans from them, or be thinking up ideas on how to improve metrics and data quality. This required hard and deep thought, meetings and often just a pen and piece of paper. I was not familiar with this to start with, however as time went on it became second nature.

There seemed no way to measure progress because as such there was no singular 'task' to complete and it was more about ensuring things were done correctly. I did not need to necessarily worry about execution of the plans that I had made, this usually was for someone else, but it did help having been in their shoes before to know in advance that my decisions were not going to encounter downstream issues.

Another thing I noted when working at a sponsor, is that you are another span of control away from the ground force. A bit like watching a football match from one side of the stadium, and you need to use aids to know exactly where the ball was and figuring out what was happening at the other end of the pitch. If a sponsor is utilising a CRO, to make something happen at the site level, you often have to go through the management and then the CRA in order for them to speak with the site. A skill which came in very handy was that of influence and clear communication, since if I could get my message across clearly, I knew that this would feed all the way through the layers of control to the site. I always saw things from the perspective of the site and patients which really helped me think about how that would translate back up to me. Whether it was to decide by close of play so that the site did not need to wait another month to meet regulatory timelines, or if it were to write a manual in a site friendly manner, I knew a lot would be riding on me. Often, I would need to rethink and go back to the drawing board.

All the eyes are on you

A big advantage to working in a sponsor is that they usually own the initial product licence after successful clinical trials. Many sponsors can be found on the stock market and are publicly listed which means the pressure to deliver not only becomes an internal challenge but an external display of brilliance. Often a benefit given by these companies is an offering of stocks which can be vested over a fixed period. This is not only motivational, but it is a great way to instil a long term drive in employees to deliver. Quite often I would find myself making it a routine to check the stock trends at the end of each day, seeing the public reaction to the company and the interest in our business activity, not least to say how much money I had potentially made. Just think about all those nice treats to buy!

With such a high stake on any one drug within a pipeline and with multiple clinical trials running together, it is common place for sponsors to publish press releases at key milestones during a trial or to announce business changes. These are periodic and often triggered by significant events. It was always interesting to watch the share price go up and down based on the latest press releases and to read the analysts reviews on my company. I had a unique perspective by contributing to the company's success through my work and also theoretically to the share price. I remember learning so much about this and looking back to when I first joined and not having known anything about how this all worked.

With plenty of eyes on sponsor companies, on top of all the regulatory bodies, there were many stakeholders and shareholders who had a strong interest. It can feel like you are walking down a catwalk. It was always important to keep your head up, keep them up to date and to hold yourself accountable for your actions. The pressure to meet target dates and to reach milestones was real and ensuring that there were no roadblocks on the path to success was important. I learnt that the best way to deal with the external environment, the internal pressure and the spotlight was to focus on my own role, tasks and challenges to ensure they were completed, accounted for and consistent. Only then would each employees' goals add up to help achieve the company's objectives.

I remember the sheer number of stakeholders involved in the study that I was working on. There were vendors left right and centre. Managing each of them and keeping an eye on the site management piece was a real challenge. The area of work I had spent most of my energy previously now formed only a small piece of the larger picture that would be a clinical trial. I was amazed and appreciated the sheer complexity within each function. Thinking of all the challenges put together, it's a miracle that a clinical trial could ever be conducted, yet alone, going through various amendment cycles and get completed – but it does!

Top Tips

#1 - Prepare for a change of pace. If you are joining a sponsor from a CRO or site or even if it is your first role, there is certainly something to note about the perspective, atmosphere and way of working that stands out as being different.

#2 - Adapt your way of working to fit the tools, resources and information available to you. It's often tempting to directly email or call external people to find out information, however sponsors are often provided with regular reports and tools to use to find out what they need. Therefore, it is important to contact people directly if there is something specific or urgent to address.

#3 - Think carefully about your choices when deciding if you want to work for a smaller sponsor or a larger one. There can be big differences in your experience, and it all depends on what skills you want to gain.

#4 - Ensure you have plenty of spare paper and time to think hard about plans, decisions and strategies. There are times where you will need to think of a new process or develop a strategy for a new initiative.

#5 - If you have had the privilege of working at a site or CRO, always ensure to use your experience and bring up hurdles, challenges and roadblocks that may not have been thought about when something is being decided. Always think about how things will look like from each different perspective.

#6 - Always be aware of the overall timelines, company plans and targets. Often the work that you do is centred around a planned announcement or target date, so its good to know what is happening to ensure that you are not caught out by surprise.

#7 - Things can change more than you think. A sponsor makes many of the decisions about a clinical trial, therefore the tendency to change deadlines or to implement or alter aspects of the trial is common. Make sure that these can be communicated thoroughly to all relevant stakeholders as the changes are worthless if they do not trickle down to the people that really need to be aware of them.

#8 - If you are working on a fully outsourced study, remember that there is a CRO working in the background for you. Importantly, be aware of what is going on within the CRO so having a great relationship and oversight of your vendors is vital in delivering your study on time and to budget.

#9 - If you are working within trial management be prepared for potentially attending numerous meetings. Your calendar will easily fill up so block time out for tasks and breaks.

#10 - You will often be working across multiple time zones, therefore be prepared for early starts or late calls, there really is no simple solution to ensuring you can meet with your teams and sites. Also prepare for longer haul travel or a greater need for accompanied visits at certain times.

Chapter 4 – Being a Clinical Research Associate (CRA)

Why become a CRA?

Quite often you will hear many people in the industry refer to the "CRA". First, I had no idea who a CRA was or even what the acronym was an abbreviation for. After working at a site and finding out that it was for a 'Clinical Research Associate', things became clearer. Prior to the use of the acronym, these individuals were traditionally called 'monitors', and no, not the sort that is attached to a computer, but monitors for the progress of a study at a site. Nowadays, even the title has moved on and some may be referred to as Site Managers, which encompasses broader responsibilities within a holistic site management role.

After hearing so much about CRAs and eventually getting an opportunity to work with them whilst at site, the role became attractive to me and since many of them visit different investigator sites, the perks of travel and the excitement that it brings was something I had always wanted in a career. Secondly, I felt that it was a role which required multi-disciplinary skills, from being able to present, looking at details in the data, through to interacting with sites whilst having oversight of the different components of the trial. Most importantly I also knew that this was a key role in being able to progress my career in future, since monitoring is a key and critical function of being able to conduct commercial research.

When I eventually became a CRA it was a great relief, and I could not wait to get out on the road and start monitoring studies. I knew that there would be a detailed training programme and when I started, on my first day I was set up with essential gadgets and tools required for the job such as a brand-new company car, laptop, scanner and phone, all of which were massive bonuses to me at the time. It felt like I had won the lottery and yet I hadn't done any work yet! Eventually, I was assigned a study and the real work began, it was a very daunting experience as you do not fully appreciate the number of tasks and challenges you will face when on a visit. The job really starts as soon as you leave your house, and the challenges begin way before that. Quite often I had to plan how I was going to get to the site, what time to leave the house and to top it all, when there were delays and cancellations to travel it was a nightmare to keep things to schedule. Even finding the clinic within the hospital was a challenge, often I remember going around in circles at a site despite visiting it a few times – you will be surprised how all sites seem as one eventually!

Many people I spoke to were also quite the opposite to me and did not want to move into that role which was their own choice. They would say things like "I wouldn't mind being a one, it's just the travel I can't deal with". Due to the highly demanding travel component of the role, it is not everyone's cup of tea especially if you have commitments outside of work, and there are other options such as roles as a Clinical Monitoring Associate (CMA) which essentially is a remote CRA, but in my opinion nothing can beat the full experience. Only after becoming a competent CRA did I realise why it was such a prestigious and sought-after role. It was an exciting job and it lived up to be everything I had hoped it would be.

"But it's impossible to get my first CRA Job"

It is a great role to be a **CRA**, so it should be straight forward to get into the role with some prior experience in research, right? Wrong! I, like many others were queuing at the edge of the cliff looking across to the brilliance of 'CRA land' across the other side but also seeing the huge gap that requires taking that gigantic leap of faith to get there. Unlike many roles where transitioning between them can be done easily and smoothly, the role is unique and quite different which makes demonstrating your competence very difficult. Despite having shadowed many, performed some in house monitoring tasks and winning an "Aspiring CRA" award at an international competition, I was still not a worthy candidate in many cases.

The keywords and key experience required when recruiters are looking for is "do you have any on-site monitoring experience?" or "How many years of on-site monitoring experience do you have?". This sounded strange since the roles I applied for were the entry-level positions and I often found myself questioning how I could get experience monitoring on site when I needed the job to be able to do that, and it was not that I could just take this as additional work since the role required travel and full assignment to a project. The level of monitoring exposure and shadowing experience I had demonstrated did not quite cut it with the recruiters. Also, because there are just so many candidates aspiring for that role, the competition is high. I

57

continued searching and saw endless positions for CRA II (mid level), and Senior CRA, however there was only a handful of CRA I (junior) roles. A common way that people take on the role is to get onto an internal training programme within a CRO who will train you to the required standard and then ease you into a junior position when a project assignment becomes available. Larger companies can do this easily due to the variety of projects they manage and therefore there is a higher chance of a less complex and straight forward trial on offer. But often, sponsors want at a minimum of mid-level and Senior staff working on their studies.

I found that my organisation's training programme was not going to be running the year I had planned to become a CRA. My chances were to either wait until the following year which was not guaranteed or to seek opportunities elsewhere. Both options were challenging, but I persisted and with a little preparation and a bit of luck thrown in a unique opportunity came about. One day I decided to add different recruiters at companies to my mobile network, some being from larger CROs and simply reached out to some asking about opportunities. I had not realised how many I was missing whilst carrying out this activity. Many companies I had applied to already had my CV, but one particular message received stated that they would forward my request to the relevant recruiter. I thought nothing of it, and then, just as I was going off to lunch, I received an email titled "CRA I Job Application" to my surprise, mainly because it was so rare to see such jobs listed but also because the actual application and invitation to apply was detailed within the email. This role was not even advertised on the company's website, so this time I really did not hesitate to complete the forms. After taking a telephone interview I awaited in anticipation for the all important invite for a face-to-face interview. I admit, the wait was long, but my mind was pre-occupied in getting ready for the gala awards ceremony for an international researcher competition I managed to get to the finals for. On the night I won the Aspiring Clinical Research Associate Award and that added a great string to my bow. The following day I even had the interview I had been waiting for. I learnt that the Director of the department saw me at the event so was already aware of my application for the role, it seemed that being on stage at that moment was a game changer after all! I was offered the position and could not wait to start. Mine is an example of a unique but rare way someone gets to a CRA position. What was your route like? If you are just starting off on your search only time will tell how easy it will be.

To give credit to the tough process, it was only after starting to perform the role did I realise why the experience, and requirements are so demanding. The role is worth all the struggle, but it will feel great when your feet land firmly on the other side of the gap after taking that leap of faith.

Once I am a CRA it will be plain sailing

After researching the role so much during the application stages, there was one thing I knew for certain, that once I was there it really was just plain sailing after that. Boy, was I wrong again! Many a time you would see people switching between companies, progressing to senior level or ending up into a project management role after becoming a lead CRA. Once you have monitoring experience your progression can be straight forward, if you develop your skills and experience in site management and monitoring as you sort of end up becoming part of an elite group of clinical research professionals. This automatically puts you at an advantage with similar jobs, and almost all the time the supply of CRAs is smaller than the demand so the moves can be lucrative.

As you embark on a CRA career, learning all the new skills, going on site, travelling, juggling the multiple priorities really takes time to master. It felt overwhelming at times, and almost like training in the circus, you get there eventually! Getting into the flow of spending half your time on the road, as well as problem solving with sites is what made the role enjoyable and varied for me. It was not as simple as people who had performed the role for a while made out to be. Just like learning to drive, it is such a new skill that you feel you will never master it, yet after many years it becomes second nature – I cannot think of any better example of the feeling of freedom you get afterwards.

As my career progressed, it was great that I had managed to demonstrate sufficient experience to become a CRA II (mid level). It was partly due to on site experience, but much of the levelling depends on how you holistically manage a clinical trial at your sites as well as the work you do which demonstrates key competencies for the role. I remember thinking to myself that many people are mistaken when they assume that to get up the ladder as a CRA you need to be on site every day of the week, write more reports than having hot dinners whilst trying to meet key metrics. The effort and experience certainly count but it is more the quality of the work, the overall health of your sites and studies that will make you stand out from the crowd as competent.

On the other end of the spectrum when I was ready to disembark from the role and take the common route into clinical trial management, the same gap in experience felt when becoming a CRA for the first time was present again, however if you go via the senior or lead route things would be a little easier. You can begin to take on additional tasks to build experience and once you have demonstrated competence the management roles become more within reach. Its quite the opposite to taking on monitoring experience, since management roles tend to be more desk based and therefore it's easier to assist and gain experience on the job. There are roles that you can take as an Associate Trial Manager or you may decide to go into a completely different area of research. The role really does give you valuable skills and experience to take your career in any direction and I have seen so many colleagues change course or even industry! The key to overcoming many of the challenges and to make your journey plain sailing, is to keep building up experience in the direction of travel you wish your career to head.

Have your passports and suitcases ready

One of the biggest aspects of being a CRA is the extensive travel that the role requires. It makes sense, right? If you are running a large scale 'experiment' then you need to be physically at the place where all the action is happening to coordinate and ensure things are going to plan. This is not something that can be fully managed from a desk miles away but technology advances are slowly allowing this to become more common. I would be assigned to sites within one country or region. Most roles are national but there are roles that are regionalised. These regionalised roles tend to mean CRAs may take on more studies naturally, to ensure they can cover the department's workload within the region.

I remember going on my first visit, it was exciting! I had to book a hotel and a train journey, and I remember not being able to sleep the day before. Corporate systems are usually set up in a way that makes booking travel easy as well as using the same system to claim the expenses back at the end of a visit. I was fortunate to also hold a corporate credit card which I could use to keep my transactions for work separate to my personal ones. A considerable amount of time and effort is required to book travel. After a while it becomes second nature like most things, but it certainly is important as the last thing you want after a long journey is to turn up to a hotel having booked the wrong one or date, let alone wasting company money. Luckily, this never happened to me, but I do recall once making the schoolboy error of not collecting a receipt during my first visit! I signed up to many travel schemes and incentives where you could collect points for stays at a hotel. I really began to enjoy my job and got use to the regular patterns of travelling to the same sites and hotels, then started to pick out my own favourites. The same went for the towns and cities I visited. There were locations where day trips were possible and others where I had to stay overnight. It was certainly strange at first walking around the town or nearby the hotel to find a restaurant and asking for a table for one. Luckily, I lived near a major train station interchange, airport and major motorway which helped with the role; however, a consideration would be how connected your home location is for travel, let's face it, a CRA will be travelling nearly every week.

There were some weeks where I covered over 1500 miles in travel, being at opposite ends of the country in the space of a week whilst squeezing in a visit to the office in-between. The excitement was great and since I loved being in different locations and exploring, the role was perfect. On the flip side, there were days that I had to set my alarm for 4am, and not return home until 7pm or later at times. The long days, intense monitoring activities on site, as well as travel can be tiresome, so it is vital that you rest to allow you to be ready for the next visit. I often found it helpful to claim back time where I had worked over during the same week if possible; rest is always better at the time when you need it most, not four weeks later!

There was a particular site located in the middle of nowhere that I needed to fly over to. The experience of flying as a normal part of your job, with all the airport checks, waiting around and passport controls thrown in as an extra to your already busy schedule is something to get accustomed to. I often flew in a propeller aircraft which had space for about 20 passengers. It was an experience and a half, and I always had a story to tell when I returned to the office. I remember sympathising with associates in countries like the US or Australia where flying was the only practical mode of travel. Packing was also a regular activity, one thing I ensured was having a pre-packed bag so that I only had to add in a few items each time I travelled. Having to rock up at a site with the wrong socks or even worse no trousers was a real worry!

After returning from a trip, there is always that task of reclaiming expenses. Luckily, this was made easy using specialist systems and software to capture receipts, I looked forward to receiving any money owed to me, but one thing was for sure the pile of receipts sure did stack up eventually, but by the end of my CRA career I finally got rid of them.

Top Tips

#1 - Prepare for extensive travel. There is no doubt that you will be spending a lot of time on the road. Sign up to travel reward clubs and ensure you have a good reliable car.

#2 - Ensure you can have a pre-packed bag or checklist. The last thing you want is to forget an essential item simply because you were in a hurry to pack.

#3 - Get to know your sites well. It is important to ask the site questions which start "tell me how..." or "How do you...". Keep asking these questions to get to the depths of a site process. You will be surprised how much hidden knowledge and insight is provided when you probe the site.

#4 - Make sure you have a good site map or directions. Often sites merge into one in your mind, and it can be confusing to find and remember clinic locations. Downloading a site map or having the coordinators phone number to hand is very handy when you are walking around site with no internet signal.

#5 - Be prepared to work in the strangest of places. From basements to broom cupboards anywhere that there is space, or where a desk will be on offer. If you're lucky you may get a room with a view or window. It may be that you also share a space with other CRAs. Also remember that if a space is not suitable for monitoring in, then raise this with the site or your manager, after all it is your workplace for the day and must still be suitable for you.

#6 – Expect change and be flexible. Sites and doctors are busy and often plans will change. Be prepared to rearrange meeting slots or to have less time than planned for meeting the Principal Investigator.

#7 – Find a good location to write your monitoring reports. In the chaos of travel, planning visits and attending to site problems you need to focus on writing up a report. It can be helpful to close your emails or to reduce distractions whilst writing as it will mean you can complete your reports more quickly and will be able to focus.

#8 – If you are struggling to find a CRA role, try to gain as much exposure or experience with monitoring or site management as you can. Network with others to ask about their routes into the role or try to stand out from the crowd to get the attention of recruiters and hiring managers.

#9 – Always try to build experience in line with your development goals. It is very difficult to break into the trial management space if this is something you intend to do. If it is another area, then also try to gain as much experience on the job as you can. After all there are typically more CRAs than study managers, so you need to be able to demonstrate experience.

#10 – Work closely with other CRAs and try to gain experience going to other visits than to your own. This will help you to pick up new techniques ideas or ways of working that you can incorporate into your own style. It's surprising how things you never thought of could be of so much benefit.

Chapter 5 –
Healthcare in the
Community & Beyond

My career really began since graduating from university after completing a bachelor and master's degree. Before I headed into the world of drug development and research to help the industry with the overall aim to improve lives and give people hope of a better future, I had experienced healthcare on the front line. Seeing the 'end products' of research being handed out to patients or working with those suffering health conditions, really gave me a broader understanding of how healthcare in the community functioned and interfaced with other services.

I remember starting off volunteering in a local hospital, conducting patient satisfaction surveys on the ward. I was given a clipboard and pen, to then later be let loose within the hospital for a couple of hours to gather as much data from inpatients as possible. I used this opportunity to explore the many different wards, often observing medics doing their job and at the same time talking with patients about their stay, how good they found the food or staff. Sometimes I would attend over two months and see some of the same patients there, at other times I would see patients move between wards. The experience was a great eye opener into how wards functioned and what patients really wanted, even if that was down to the flavour of jam on their toast! I also spent time shadowing doctors directly both in hospitals and the community, as well as surgeons in theatre to really get a deep insight into the different treatment pathways.

Another large part of my year in the community was focussed on the care setting. I volunteered at a care home for residents with dementia doing arts and crafts each week. It was a fantastic way to appreciate the work of healthcare staff in homes and to see the enormous effort it takes to make a care home function. I also remember enjoying meeting the other volunteers regularly and planning out our activities together for the residents. It was a challenge communicating with some of the residents due to their condition and from time to time they would forget who you were during the same session. Some of the residents did not realise where they were or felt they were still back home doing what they used to do. It was a privilege to contribute to their cognitive health and to stimulate their minds through the power of art and craft. I did learn a few new design hacks myself!

To fill in the gaps and earn some money, I began a part time job in a large community pharmacy chain. It was great to get some income, but more so, I was fortunate to be able to work for a qualification as a Medicine Counter Assistant. I learnt about remedies for certain types of common symptoms that customers would ask me about and the course allowed me to gain an understanding of how over the counter medicines worked. I remember meeting our regular customers and getting to know them, even their habits! Working so closely with the Pharmacist, I was able to really get involved in assisting them with their role, handing out prescriptions and processing them for dispensing. It was fascinating to witness the broad range of medications that were being prescribed in the community and there were some common themes. I was also able to retain the knowledge which was useful during my degree.

Another area of the community which is always open for help is the charity sector. I was fortunate to fill my time volunteering in a charity shop that funded research for people living with heart conditions. I remember processing donations and getting them onto the shop floor as well as assisting customers with purchases. It was great to play a direct role in the collection of funds for vital clinical research and it was a satisfying experience. I can say that my skills in ironing and organising stacks of donations were really put to the test!

Much of what I experienced was an eye opener into the inter-connected healthcare that takes place within the community, whether that was directly with doctors in hospitals, or through care homes, or charity shops. This perspective really boosted my outlook, and I would recommend volunteering to anyone able to fit this into their lives.

In addition to the community work I also recall the vast amount of learning that took place through the interviewing process for roles. I had applied for a particular placement and was called for an interview. Ahead of the grilling, I was fortunate to be given a detailed tour inside a drug manufacturing plant. I remember being amazed as I had never seen anything like it before. I had to gear up in protective wear, decontaminate and then walk through the plant. It was like being in a Sci-Fi film with rooms along a big corridor with wall to floor doors opening, making that "pressurised air release" sound when opening! I was also fortunate to visit a Contract Manufacturing Organisation (CMO) in the far north and spent time with the scientists who were using techniques and lab equipment that I had only ever learnt about as theory at university; it was just fascinating to see things in reality. I took this experience back with me to visualise and understand my university work with a greater depth of understanding. Even though I did not get the role, I took away some great insights as well as a smile.

Chapter 6 – Perks, pathways and specialist functions

I work in an industry where I can wake up excited to make a difference each day. Research work is equally varied and challenging and can be very fulfilling in the knowledge that the end goal is making a difference to patients lives. With all of that in mind, there are also other obvious common reasons for us working in this industry. For example, getting a good income, being able to pay our bills, to feel empowered to do our best and working with colleagues in a collaborative environment, and having the benefits from the tools provided to perform our roles. I class all these as 'perks of the job', and it is something that is very important to consider when choosing a company to work for.

I remember one of my first interviews when I was asked why I wanted to work for that company. I started giving a speech about how great their firm was, the number of awards they had won and the products they had helped bring to market. There was a silence. Then I was asked, "well, why not work next door at our competitor as I can tell you they have achieved more than us?". The question was thought provoking, and it made me realise that they had made a good point. It was after looking back on this experience I appreciated that the key differentiator between companies is their culture, people and soft touches which make them appealing over another. It is the way that their values fit with your own that determine how you will fit in. Of course, the reputation of the company and its achievements play a part, but they are not the only differentiators sometimes.

Another aspect to think about when joining a company or taking on a new role is that of personal development. You may be content at where you are and have no intention to progress which is fine, or you may want to become the next CEO. Either way, there is always room for development within any role whether that is to learn a new skill, develop a new process or become a better person. Knowing about the different training options, routes and development support that is on offer at any given company is crucial in being able to succeed with them. Remember that the company operates as a business that needs to make profit and sometimes that business gets in the way of things. In clinical research there are many career paths and entry points, therefore knowing and researching them before hand will be wise. I outline some of these broad areas and my experiences with them, however there are so many more avenues. For example, you could focus on patient recruitment, trial coordination, monitoring, data, or safety to name a few. The main path I took was within operations which tends to feed into all the other main functions.

Clinical Operations

Without Clinical Operations, clinical trials would simply not take place. That sounds a little biased, but I truly believe it! This department tends to form one of the largest functions which essentially plans, tracks and implements the trial procedures in the real world setting and ensures that the study protocols, regulations and study objectives and endpoints can be met and kept on track. Internally, the Clinical Operations teams pull together cross functional activities and act as a central point of coordination. This ensures that any decisions or activities can be implemented at clinical sites on time and to budget. Roles can vary from trial coordination, study set up, monitoring to clinical operations leadership. This department has one of the most contacts with sites and research staff on the ground and can host a very strong career pathway into project and trial management. I have spent much of my time in this department and have often felt the strong energetic atmosphere within it. The highs and lows of site activity really feeds into this function and the dynamic aspect to the work that goes on within Clinical Operations made no two days the same.

Data Management

Without data to support any new product there is no product. Data Management is a very important and crucial function which is focussed primarily on ensuring the data deliverables are met. They form a function to plan, implement, transfer and design data sets between clinical systems and provide a service during the trial to ensure that data is accurate and in line with study plans. Analysing data trends and ensuring consistency and reliability also form a large part of this function. These teams get involved with the protocol design and meeting other departments to ensure that key deliverables are incorporated into data collection or processing activities. The function provides varied career routes. I often interacted with data management teams, especially as a CRA when data queries would arise, or database locks were imminent. There is a depth of information that data management hold for any study and sometimes it was always nice to meet with the team on a one-to-one basis to get this insight which is usually only summarised.

Medical Affairs

The Medical Affairs function is a crucial one that bridges industry with the wider medical community. The department manages external relationships with key medical staff, scientists and experts in any given specialism. They act as a go-between to ensure that the latest medical practice and learning can be incorporated into new products or development programs and to educate clinical sites on any useful study insights. Many individuals within the department are therefore qualified medical practitioners or hold PhD qualifications at a minimum. Roles vary and range from Medical Information, to Medical Science Liaisons, to Medical Affairs Directors. I only really interacted strongly with this function when working in a smaller sponsor. The ability to link with these professionals was valuable and the insights that they brought were fascinating. I often felt like I was back at university listening to a keynote speaker or lecture, but only this time, I had to pay special attention and use the information to bring about real change to a study's trajectory.

Regulatory Affairs

The Regulatory Affairs teams have a vital role in ensuring that any clinical trial complies with regulatory guidelines, and that any changes to the study can be incorporated in line with specific country requirements; a bit like being able to drive a car in one country, but then having to qualify in each other country globally to do the same thing elsewhere. They serve as an interface between the regulatory authorities and the study teams to manage the communication of changes required to a study, as well as obtaining approval for new documents and procedures that are to be implemented. The regulatory environment is very complex and there are many intricate aspects to the function. It also provides a host of career opportunities within this specialism and gives good exposure to the practices within research in different countries. I think that anyone managing global regulatory affairs deserves a gold medal, it really is not easy! I remember joining my first calls with the team and I was so lost in the complexities and intricacies. After getting a grip and overview of the processes, it was interesting to see how simple document updates or small changes could impact an entire regulatory submission or strategy and the detrimental impact to timelines that this had.

Pharmacovigilance

This department can also be referred to as drug safety. The teams collect, analyse, monitor and aim to prevent adverse effects of drugs and therapies. It is a very scientific and process driven area within the

80

industry. There is also a large regulatory component to the work within pharmacovigilance, as many adverse effects are required to be reported to authorities which varies between countries. Often the department deals with a vast amount of processing and therefore being able to work to strict reporting timelines and having a good understanding of safety reporting procedures is essential. One thing that I did take away was that they were often a group of very hard-working people. Frequently, once a site enters or provides information about adverse reactions, we do not appreciate the mountain of work behind the scenes that goes on which allows these to be reconciled and reported. Truly fascinating!

Logistics & Supplies

If patients cannot get the study drug in their hands, then equally there cannot be a study. The distribution of supplies from the manufacturing plants through to distribution centres, to countries and to site involves a chain of people, stakeholders and authorities. There is a large element of being able to plan and foresee future events in advance to ensure supply shortages and delays do not impact the study progress, as well as being able to track and monitor the status of different suppliers and stakeholders in the process. Being a varied department has its own challenges. It is often too easy to accept deliveries at site or to request for a new supply of drug if they are running low, however there is much more that goes on behind the scenes. I remember learning about supply strategies, small changes with supply vendors that required out of the box thinking and collaboration across functions, to ensure we could continue the study amidst all the challenges. Often you do not see the physical products or supplies moving around, but to be able to imagine this and visualise the physical movement globally with the loading and unloading of boxes and packages always helps me to realise the sheer impact and importance of this function on a trial.

Business Development & Management

For those that have an interest in general management, the field of research, or if you want to gain insight into how whole companies operate, the business and management functions within pharmaceutical and CRO companies can provide a wealth of experience. You may be able to work with new business proposals or with vendors. Similarly, you may want to manage reporting, support project managers or study teams and even get involved with business strategy. Equally, many people move from clinical functions to focus more on a role that is weighted towards business. These roles can exist within each function as well as separately within a business development function depending on each company's structure. I often interacted with Project Managers, Administration and Business development when it came to providing me with all things report related, HR or new business. Quite often the sheer number of supporting functions was mind boggling and to think that there are dedicated teams working on such specific tasks, especially within a CRO was insightful.

There is a world of opportunity and cross functional areas in clinical research. I strongly believe that there is a role to suit everyone's skills and strengths, so, it is always great to consult with the experts in the industry as I did before making any big decisions.

Chapter 7 – Where next, and the future of the clinical research industry

Admittedly I have enjoyed the benefits of making rapid progression through the early stages of my career and being able to experience the many different aspects of research in different settings has certainly been truly fascinating. There are still many avenues and options open to me that I have yet to explore, however a career is to be considered a marathon as opposed to a sprint. The pace may slow but as you reach to new heights, it is the experience and quality time within a function or role that will really count. The advantage of being able to witness the different environments in succession, meant that my experiences were still fresh at each stage. I hope to continue to progress within trial management, but let us see what the future holds! One thing for sure is that I will always seek out elements of travel, working closely with sites, CROs and doctors in any future role.

Clinical Research as an industry is always booming. Not a year has gone by without new products, pipelines and trials opening. There is always going to be a new study, disease or health crisis to tackle. The triumph with the development of coronavirus vaccines is a true example of this. I think that the industry can offer great career prospects, skills and satisfaction in any role. Ultimately, we each work for the benefit of patients. With a rapidly changing healthcare environment we have already seen many companies changing alongside to better meet client's needs as well as to ensure patients can receive new treatments without many hurdles along the way. To this effect I believe mergers and acquisitions will continue to dominate the industry, with CROs becoming even larger and better able to run studies globally. Having stated that, it will open more opportunity for smaller firms to fill any niche gaps that this may create in the market. There will be a greater focus on virtual trials with an increasing number of patient site visits being replaced with home health care instead. I think there will also be a greater role for organisations to keep innovating within the industry or to provide more tailored solutions for clients and patients. It is going to be an exciting time!

Technology may also play a large role in being able to better manage clinical research studies, and with that may come a host of new roles and positions that perhaps have never existed before. The pharmaceutical sponsor companies and healthcare decision makers may also work more collaboratively in a new connected fashion from the early development stages of products, to ensure that they can be expedited to patients for use. This way of working may also underline the importance of tackling rare disease and highlight areas where there is currently no cure or treatment option. I am no mystic meg, but there have been discussions of these changes coming for a while, so it really is a matter of time before we start to see big changes. Either way there will always be something new to consider! Perhaps another edition of my book will be required in future to see what more insight I can uncover and if I was right or wrong?

Chapter 8 – The Patient

All too often, after a frantic working day, long meetings and numerous problems encountered during a typical working week, the patient can sometimes get out of focus, especially for those not working at a site. If it were not for patients there would be many who would not have a job to do. So, it is important to keep the patient at the heart of every decision, process and trial. It is great to see more companies now adopting a patient first culture within their organisation.

So, who is the patient? Put simply, it is anyone at any time that can become a patient. In the world of research, they can also be referred to as the participant or subject of research and is the real focal point of any new drug discovery project.

During procedural visits, the trial patient will meet with doctors or specialists and it will feel for them as though the research is part of their routine care. They may have additional procedures and tests and will ultimately visit the site frequently, but it is knowingly for the benefit of science and the greater medical attention they receive is all part of a clinical trial. I have been involved as a contributor to a research paper where we investigated the types of participants and their engagement with clinical trials. One of the significant findings was that in general, patients found they were well informed about the process before taking part in any new trial. What was surprising to me was that it became evident patients wanted to be involved in not just the trial as a participant, but as part of the team designing the study procedures by providing their input. This would ensure the clinical trials were 'patient friendly'. I am glad that this is now a big part of research as we know it today, with patient participant involvement schemes and advocacy groups.

When a new drug is being developed, it is important to understand that the results should be representative of the populations that they are intended for and should show effectiveness across all types of people and demographics. With the global coronavirus pandemic and vaccine rollout in 2021, it has highlighted the greater need for certain groups to be encouraged to take up the vaccine and to participate in the trials. Without a representative trial population, it is very difficult to determine the wider benefits of any new drug brought to market. Patients in a clinical trial should feel confident that they become part of a highly regulated industry and that there are multiple layers of safety reporting and oversight in any given trial. On top of this, there is always a study doctor at each site assigned that will have the needs of the patient as their first and foremost priority. Before anyone is enrolled into a clinical trial there is a thorough consenting process and they always have a right to withdraw their consent at any time point.

As the industry moves with the times, there is now more focus on turning to remote or virtual visits. Some studies I have heard about are opening as 'site-less', and the use of virtual visits, home health and smart technology is beginning to boom. As healthcare systems and hospitals become more pressured and stretched for resources, it is only natural progression that we will see more therapies developed to fit with these healthcare systems which will not require inpatient hospital care, that are oral medicines and that can be tested in the comfort of a patient's home.

With all that considered, the role of the patient in a clinical trial will ultimately continue to evolve, as will the types of treatments and methods of conducting research.

The future for all of us looks bright!

Glossary

Adverse Reactions	An untoward reaction to an investigational product which can be related to it.
Clinical Monitoring Associate (CMA)	A person usually conducting remote activities with sites to check the quality of data, safety of participants and compliance with the study protocol.
Clinical Research Associate (CRA)	A person conducting visits to a research site to check the quality of data, safety of participants and compliance with the study protocol.
Contract Manufacturing Organisation (CMO)	An organisation that is contracted by another in the pharmaceutical industry which typically provides services in drug manufacturing.
Contract Research Organisation (CRO)	An organisation which is contracted by a another to conduct activities on

	their behalf in clinical research
Database Lock	An event where all the data entry in a study database can no longer be changed and can then be used for analysis.
Dispensing	The provision of drugs or medicines as set out properly on a lawful prescription
Good Clinical Practice (GCP)	An international quality standard, which governments can then transpose into regulations for clinical trials involving human subjects
Human Resources (HR)	The personnel of a business or organisation, regarded as a significant asset in terms of skills and abilities.
National Health Service (NHS)	The Government funded medical and health care services that everyone living in the UK can use without being asked to pay the full cost of the service.

Principal Investigator	The lead doctor responsible for the study at any given site
Research Site	A place where a clinical research study is conducted
Sponsor	An organisation that funds and has overall accountability for the conduct of a clinical trial. They usually own the rights to the product they are testing.
Trial Master File	The repository of all study documents related to a clinical trial
Virtual Trials	A remote way to conduct clinical research which may have all or a large proportion of trial procedures conducted outside of the research site.

Printed in Great Britain
by Amazon

67385174R00061